THE **CIRCLE** OF **FIFTHS**
FOR **PIANO**

Learn and Apply Music Theory for Piano & Keyboard

JOSEPH **ALEXANDER**

FUNDAMENTAL**CHANGES**

The Circle of Fifths For Piano

Learn and Apply Music Theory for Piano & Keyboard

Published by **www.fundamental-changes.com**

ISBN: 978-1-78933-019-9

Copyright © 2018 Joseph Alexander

www.fundamental-changes.com

Twitter: **@guitar_joseph**

Over 10,000 fans on Facebook: **FundamentalChangesInGuitar**

Instagram: **FundamentalChanges**

For over 350 Free Guitar Lessons with Videos Check Out

www.fundamental-changes.com

Original Circle of Fifths image inspired and adapted from Sienna Wood's great work over at www.musiccrashcourses.com

Cover Image Copyright: Shutterstock - Photojoy

Contents

Introduction

Musicians often talk about the Circle of Fifths in hushed tones as if it was some sort of Rosetta stone that provides the answers to all the mysteries of music theory.

In all honesty, they're not that far from the truth.

The Circle of Fifths, in essence is a diagram that shows the relationships between all the keys, key signatures, modulations (key changes), scales and chords in music.

Once you understand how "the Circle" is built, you have cracked its code. Once you have cracked the code, you can quickly and easily use the Circle of Fifths as a guide to writing better songs, practicing more efficiently, using interesting key changes and actually understanding how music is written.

In essence…

The Circle of Fifths forms the foundation of how *all* music works.

While figuring out how to write this book, I did some research into how other writers and musicians approach teaching the Circle. While they generally do a great job of explaining it, I'm yet to find a useful resource showing how to actually apply the Circle of Fifths as a *practical* musical tool to help you play better.

If you've read any of my other 30+ other books, you should know by now that theory is useless without knowing how to apply it. For that reason, this book is different. Not only will I show you how to build and understand the Circle of Fifths, I will show you how to *use* it in your playing and writing too.

I won't lie to you: the Circle of Fifths is a largely theoretical idea so this book will be going into a forest of quite detailed theory. I promise I'll take you there slowly and steadily, step by step, one idea at a time.

When you are done with this book, you will have mastered and internalised the fundamental rules and *conventions* of music that go back over 800 years. You will understand the relationships between:

- Key Signatures

- Keys

- How to Move to Related Keys (Modulation)

- Scales

- Chords

- Relative Minors keys

Not only that, you will be able to *use* this stuff in a *practical* way on piano to help you practice and write music more efficiently.

The one thing I want you to hold on to throughout this book is the idea that "moving chords in fifths sounds good". If you have a "Why am I learning this stuff?" moment, just remember that this theory teaches you to be a better-sounding musician.

If you get really stuck, drop me an email and I'll do my best to help you out.

Music theory is simply a way of explaining how notes, chords and scales fit together. Great composers have written beautiful music and often it is the teacher's job to try to explain how they've written it.

We don't learn theory just *because*. We learn it to get closer to understanding the music we love.

Theory *explains* music, but theory is *not* music.

For this reason, I have included many audio examples in this book that I want you to listen to. To understand music, you can't just see it on a piece of paper – you need to hear and internalise what it sounds like, and be able to relate the theory to real life sounds.

For the same reason, I strongly urge you to explore the practical musical ideas given in this book. They sow the seeds for a lifetime of creativity.

Go to **www.fundamental-changes.com/download-audio** right now and get the audio examples for this book. You'll thank me later!

OK, let's dive in!

Have fun!

Joseph

Get the Audio

The audio files for this book are available to download for free from **www.fundamental-changes.com.** The link is in the top right-hand corner. Simply select this book title from the drop-down menu and follow the instructions to get the audio.

We recommend that you download the files directly to your computer, not to your tablet, and extract them there before adding them to your media library. You can then put them on your tablet, iPod or burn them to CD. On the download page there is a help PDF and we also provide technical support via the contact form.

Kindle / eReaders

To get the most out of this book, remember that you can **double tap any image to enlarge it**. Turn off 'column viewing' and hold your kindle in landscape mode.

Twitter: **@guitar_joseph**

Over 10,000 fans on Facebook: **FundamentalChangesInGuitar**

Instagram: **FundamentalChanges**

Chapter One: Notes and Intervals

Let's start our study of the Circle of Fifths by making sure we understand the basic building blocks and terminology of music.

The smallest unit of distance in western music is a *semitone*. A semitone is the distance between each note on your piano.

If you start on the note C and ascend, playing every white and black key, you are moving in semitones.

Example 1a:

The final note you reach is the same as the first note, C. The second C is an *octave* higher than the first.

Example 1b:

In Example 1a, you actually played a scale called the *Chromatic* scale. A Chromatic scale is a scale where you play *every* semitone between two notes an octave apart. In Example 1a, you played the C Chromatic scale, however you can start on any note. If you started on the note A, you would have played the A Chromatic scale. If you started on the note D you would have played the D Chromatic scale, etc.

Here's the G Chromatic Scale.

Example 1c:

You can probably hear why the chromatic scale isn't used very much in music. It's not very melodic and doesn't have much character.

The thing to take away from this exercise is that there are *12 semitones in an octave.*

1	2	3	4	5	6	7	8	9	10	11	12	1
E	F	F#	G	G#	A	A#	B	C	C#	D	D#	E

On the piano, the C Chromatic scale looks like:

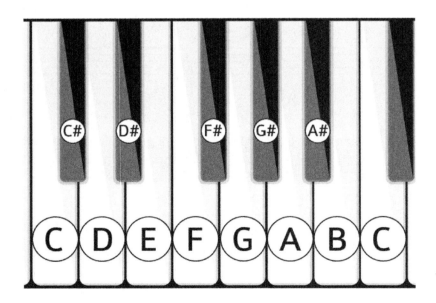

Notice that there is no # note between B and C, or E and F. Don't worry about this for now. It's just something that happens because of physics!

The next smallest unit of distance in music is a *tone*. One tone is equal to two semitones.

Start on the note C again and this time move in tones up to the octave.

Example 1d:

Repeat this from the note G.

It might seem strange that the scale jumps from D# to F. You were probably expecting the note E# to be written, but remember that the note E# is enharmonically the same as the note F.

Example 1e:

Sounds kind of weird, doesn't it?

There is a special name for a scale that moves only in tones. It is called the *Whole Tone* scale. This isn't a very imaginative name, but it is very descriptive.

We now know how to move in semitones and tones on the keyboard, but as you've heard, making scales out of *just* semitones or *just* tones sounds kind of awkward.

You may already be aware of the most common scale in music – the Major scale. The major scale (and all other scales) is made from different patterns of tones and semitones.

We will come to the major scale soon, but right now it is very important to learn what a "5th" is. After all, that's what this book is all about!

Remember that there are twelve semitones in an octave.

A 5th is simply the distance of five note names. For example:

C – D – E – F – G

With C as our starting point, we see that G is the 5th of C.

It just so happens that when you go up five note names, this distance is seven semitones.

In music, the distance between any two notes is called an *interval*.

Play the note C and count seven semitones above it. This is the note G.

Example 1f:

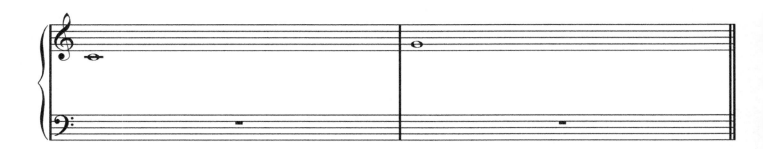

The note G is the *perfect 5th* of C.

This works on any note. Repeat the process starting on the note A and starting on the note D:

Example 1g:

An interval of a perfect 5th between the notes D and A looks like this on the piano.

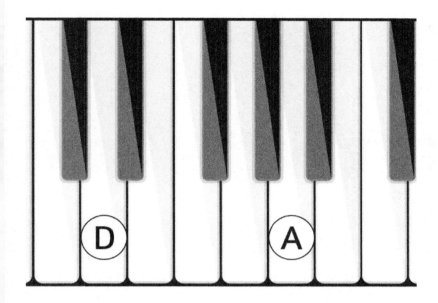

The distance from A to E is an *interval* of a *perfect 5th*.

The *interval* from D to A is a *perfect 5th*

The *interval* from G to D is a *perfect 5th*

5ths can be calculated easily by counting up five notes from the starting point.

For example:

Count up five white keys from C:

C – D – E – F – G

The note G is the perfect 5th of C.

Count up five white notes from A:

A – B – C – D – E

The distance from A to E is the interval of a perfect 5th.

A warning!

This system of counting isn't perfect because it doesn't account for sharps (#) and flats (b) so you need to be careful.

For example, you might expect the 5th of B to be F. It isn't, it is F#.

I promise you that this will become clear very soon, so don't panic. The Circle of Fifths holds all the answers and you will soon discover its secrets!

Because the spacing of the notes on a keyboard isn't symmetrical, it's useful to learn what a 5th interval looks like starting from each black key. The process is always the same if you remember that a perfect 5th contains seven semitones.

So from the note C# count up seven semitones and you arrive at G#.

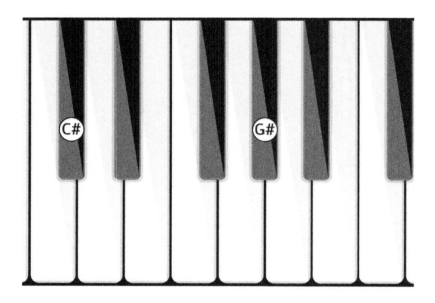

To form a perfect 5th on the note D#, count up seven semitones to arrive at A#.

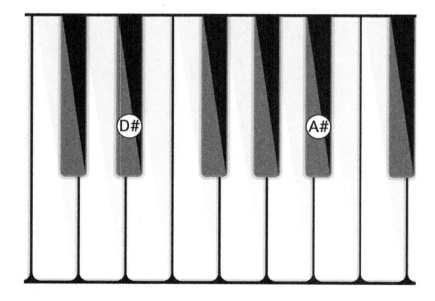

Here's F# to C#:

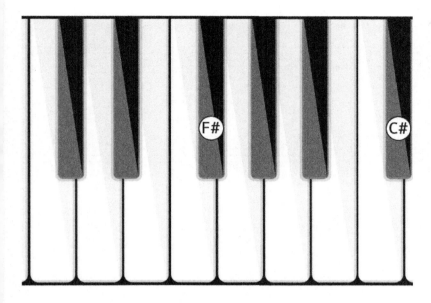

Repeat this process on the notes G# and A#.

It's important to understand that a perfect fifth can be played in any direction. For example, ascending from C to G forms the same interval as descending from C to G.

Example 1h:

Great, so what?!

Why have I taken the time to explain this so carefully?

Well, the movement of 5ths is one of the strongest, most important sounds in music. It's been used for over 800 years to help musicians write great music. It is pretty much the basis of all jazz, pop and rock.

To show you what I mean, let's play perfect 5ths ascending in tones from the note C.

Example 1i:

Notice that you land perfectly back at the starting point (the note C) after playing 12 different notes. In fact, you've just played every one of the 12 different notes in a "cycle" that brings you back to your starting point.

1	2	3	4	5	6	7	8	9	10	11	12	1
C	G	D	A	E	B	F#	C#	G#	D#	A#	E# / F	C

(Remember that there is no # between the notes E and F, so the note E# is really the note F)

Perhaps you're starting to see why this is called a Circle of Fifths. If you ascend in 5ths for long enough, you always get back to your starting point.

14

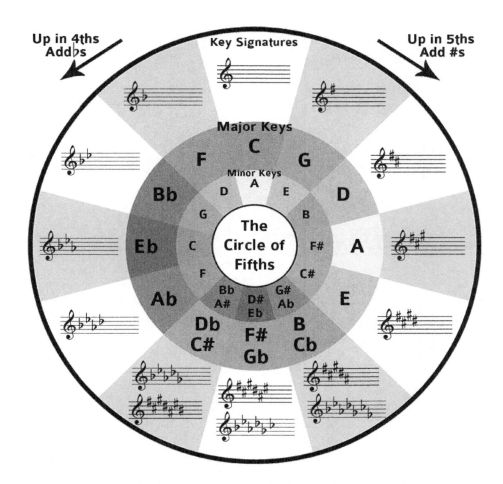

We are still just scratching the surface of the Circle of Fifths. We will be going into much greater detail in the following chapters.

For fun, let's play a major chord on each note of the above cycle. Even if you find this tricky, listen to the audio track available from **www.fundamental-changes.com/audio-downloads** to hear what this sounds like.

Some of the accidentals in the notation get pretty crazy, especially in bar three where we have to use double sharp signs (x). To help you with these chords, I've written their enharmonic equivalents above them in brackets. In practice, it's unlikely that you'll ever see an A#7 chord (for example). Bb7, however, which is enharmonically the same as A#7 crops up all the time.

If you're struggling to read or play the difficult "sharp key" chords, it will be a lot easier to think of their equivalent "flat key" chords written in brackets. Remember, E# is the same note as F!

Example 1j:

This will sound very familiar if you've ever listened to any classical music. Classical composers used the idea of moving chords in 5ths *all the time*.

Now repeat the exercise with minor chords:

Example 1k:

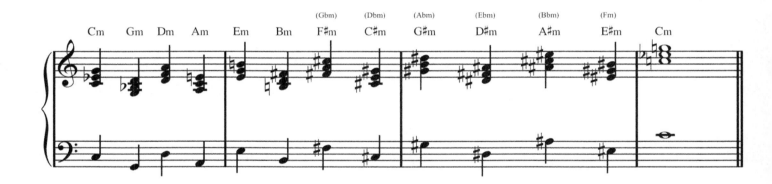

Sounds pretty dark huh?!

Now try this idea with dominant 7 chords. For simplicity I have written the E#7 chord as F7, as they are enharmonically identical.

Example 1l:

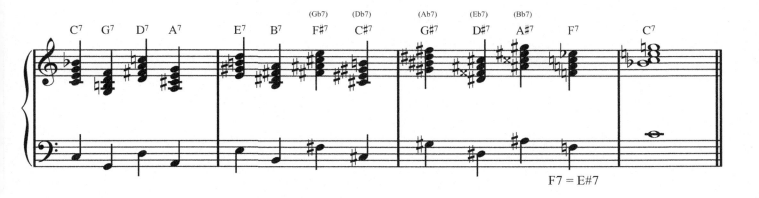

F7 = E#7

Try playing through the sequence backwards from the high C to the low C with all three types of chord.

Finally, let's *descend* (play backwards) through the sequence combining minor chords with dominant 7 chords. (Again, I've written the E#7 as an F7 chord).

Example 1m:

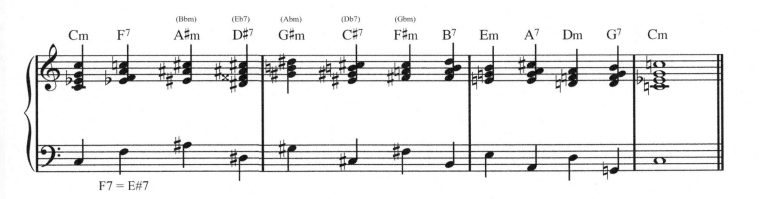

F7 = E#7

I *love* this sound. It's very common in classical music and often used in compositions. Play Example 1m again, but this time replace the Minor chords with the Major chords you used in Example 1j.

You can also switch out any minor chord for any major chord at any time. Keep playing dominant chords on every other chord and experiment with major and minor as the first chord. Then try a dominant chord as the first chord and a major or minor chord as the second.

The possibilities are endless. You can have great fun using these ideas in your own writing, chord and soloing work. If you know a bit of jazz harmony, you can start to experiment with using *altered* dominant chords too!

OK, so these examples have been a slight digression from explaining the theory of the Circle of Fifths, but remember, this is a *practical* book. You need to hear how this stuff sounds in order to fully understand it and make it your own.

Remember the basic rule: *moving in 5ths sounds good.*

I hope I have showed you some fun applications of 5ths without getting too bogged down in music theory.

You should now understand:

- The smallest distances in music are semitones and tones

- Semitones and tones are the building blocks of all scales

- The name for the distance between two notes is called an interval

- An octave interval is the distance of 12 semitones

- A 5th interval is the distance of 7 semitones

- 5ths can be played using patterns on the keyboard

- 5ths can ascend or descend

- If you keep ascending or descending in 5ths you will arrive back where you started after 12 notes

- Playing major, minor and dominant chords in 5ths sounds cool

- You can write great sequences by combining all three chord types

Pop Quiz!

What note is a 5th above C?

What note is a 5th above A?

What note is a 5th above E?

What note is a 5th above F#?

Chapter Two: Scales and Keys

A scale is a series of steps between two fixed musical points. These two fixed points are always the same note, but in different *octaves*. For example, these points could both be the note C, one being higher in pitch than the other:

Example 2a:

(Go to **www.fundamental-changes.com/audio-downloads** to get all the audio examples and backing tracks for this book).

Listen to the above example. You can hear that while the notes are fundamentally the same, they are at a different *pitch*. A scale is simply a way to break up the space in between these notes.

One way to think about this is to imagine a ladder where the first and last rungs are fixed, but you can change the spacings of any of the rungs in between. Some spaces may be smaller, some larger, but however you arrange them, after climbing the ladder you will always end up at the same fixed place.

The rungs on our ladder are the notes that we play, and the spaces between the rungs are the distances between these notes. These distances are measured in *tones* and *semitones*. Remember that two semitones are equal in distance to one tone.

It is the arrangement of the notes that makes each scale sound different, and creates a different musical feeling.

Once you have "set" the rungs of your ladder, you can carry your ladder to any different location (note) and set it down somewhere new. In the same way, any scale of the same *type* always has the same pattern of tones and semitones, no matter what your starting note is.

For example, the pattern of tones and semitones is the same whether you're playing the scale of C Major, F# Major, Bb Major or any other *major* scale.

Each scale of the same *type* (i.e. major or minor) always has the same pattern.

The Major Scale

Overview

The major scale has been the fundamental building block of Western harmony for the past 800 years. Most of the chords you hear in music can be formed from this scale. It is essential to understand how this scale works because its step pattern is the yardstick by which we describe *any* other musical sound.

Of course, the major scale is used in rock, but often its extremely happy vibe is a bit too bright for us. There are some great exceptions, however. Check out *Lean on Me* by Bill withers for a truly triumphant major feeling.

Other tunes you might want to check out, depending on your musical tastes, are:

All You Need is Love by the Beatles

Jessica by the Allman Brothers

Like a Rolling Stone by Bob Dylan

Or **Jump** by Van Halen

It is extremely important to understand how the major scale functions, and how to create melody and harmony from it before launching into the rest of this book, so make sure you are comfortable with the ideas in the following sections before moving on to part two.

Construction

Going back to our ladder analogy, we can say that the particular sound or "flavour" of the major scale is due to the way the rungs are *spaced* between the two fixed points at each end. In other words, there is a set pattern of tones and semitones that gives the major scale its unique quality. Let's discover what they are.

The best way to begin is to examine the scale of C Major. There are no sharps or flats in this scale, and if you were playing a keyboard, you would play only the white notes (no black ones) starting from and ending on the note C.

The notes in the scale of C Major are:

C D E F G A B

The note C is the *root* of the scale, often referred to as the "tonic".

The scale is easiest to see in the key of C because it doesn't include any black notes.

Example 2b:

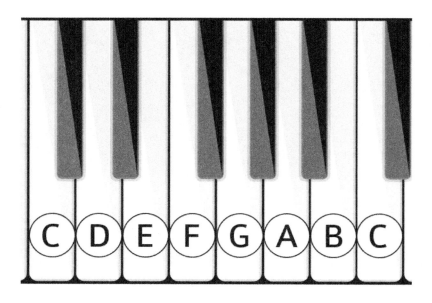

When the scale is laid out like this, it is clear to see that the distance between some notes is one tone and between others it is only semitone.

For instance, you can see the distance between C and D is one tone, and between E and F is one semitone.

Listen to and play Example 2b now. Memorise this pattern of tones and semitones as it is essential to everything that follows.

The previous diagram shows the *structure* of the major scale. Wherever we place the first note, the pattern of tones and semitones must always remain the same if we are to create the exact sound of the major scale.

The set pattern of a major scale is always:

Tone, Tone, Semitone, Tone, Tone, Tone, Semitone

C – D Tone

D – E Tone

E – F Semitone

F – G Tone

G – A Tone

A – B Tone

B – C Semitone.

Notice that the distance between the 7th note of the scale (B) and the root (C) is a semitone.

Major scales *always* have a semitone between the 7th and 1st/8th (root) of the scale. This note is called the *leading* note.

The pattern of steps **Tone, Tone, Semitone, Tone, Tone, Tone, Semitone** is not *just* the building block of the major scale. Because the major scale is so important, this pattern is really the building block of *all* music.

This is one of the most important things to know in music. Say it out loud and memorise it! I'll say it again now so it sinks in:

Tone, Tone, Semitone, Tone, Tone, Tone, Semitone.

The pattern of tones and semitones in the major scale is given its own numerical *formula*:

1 2 3 4 5 6 7

1 2 3 4 5 6 7 is the formula of the major scale.

Simple as that may seem, we can use this type of formula describe any other scale. For example, you may have seen the formula:

1 2 3 #4 5 6 7

This is a shorthand way of saying that this scale is *identical* in every way to the major scale, *except* that the 4th note has been *sharpened* by a semitone.

In the original key of C Major we had the notes,

C D E F G A B C

So the formula **1 2 3 #4 5 6 7** tells us that now the notes will be,

C D E F# G A B C

Construction of the Major Scale in Other Keys

To form the major scale in the key of C, we simply started on the note C and ran alphabetically through the notes until we got back to our starting point. Let's try this idea starting in a different place. For example, let's begin with the note G:

G A B C D E F G

We can check to see if the rungs on our ladder are the same. Remember the major scale pattern:

Tone, Tone, Semitone, Tone, Tone, Tone, Semitone.

G – A = Tone

A – B = Tone

B – C = Semitone

C – D = Tone

D – E = Tone

E – F = **Semitone**

F – G = **Tone**

You may already see that there is a problem with the pattern of tones and semitones in the final two notes. F and G.

Look back to the previous diagram and you will see that there *must* be a semitone between the 7th and final note of the scale if we are to create a proper major scale.

This is easier to see on the keyboard.

Example 2c:

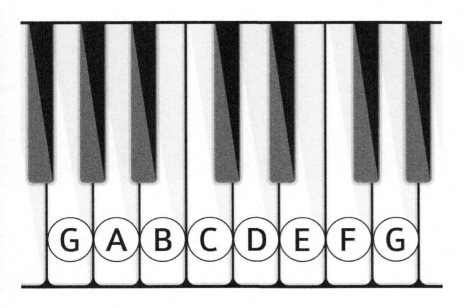

Play through this example and listen to how it sounds. Can you hear something that doesn't belong in a major scale?

Remember the major scale pattern:

Tone, Tone, Semitone, Tone, Tone, **Tone, Semitone.**

The notes from G to G above do not currently form a major scale. Their pattern is,

Tone, Tone, Semitone, Tone, Tone, **Semitone**, **Tone**.

The last rung on the ladder should be a semitone and the one before that should be a tone.

There is a very simple way to fix this problem. We simply sharpen the 7th note (F) so it becomes F# like this:

Example 2d:

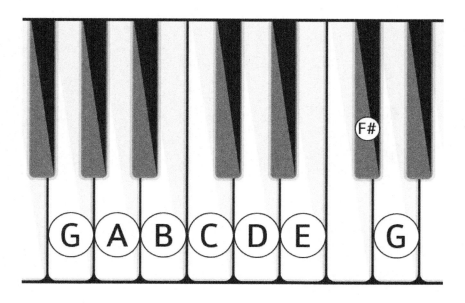

To create the major scale pattern of **Tone, Tone, Semitone, Tone, Tone, Tone Semitone,** we had to raise the 7th note of the scale by one semitone.

This G Major scale is now identical in *construction* to the C Major scale that we formed at the start of this chapter.

1 2 3 4 5 6 7

Before we raised the 7th note to F#, we could have described the scale as:

1 2 3 4 5 6 b7

We needed to raise the 7th note to make it match the major scale formula.

It was no coincidence that I chose the note G as an example to build this new major scale. It is also no coincidence that the note G is a 5th above the note C that we used in the first example.

As we move up in 5ths (from C to G, or from to D to A etc.) we can form a major scale on each new note by adding a # to the 7th note of the new scale.

We will look at this concept in much greater detail in the next chapter.

You should now understand:

- Major scales are all formed from the same pattern of tones and semitones, even though the notes in each scale may be different

- The set pattern of a major scale is *always* Tone, Tone, Semitone, Tone, Tone, Tone, Semitone

- This pattern of notes is so important it is given the *master formula* 1 2 3 4 5 6 7

- All other scales can be described by using adjustments to this formula (e.g. b3, #4 #5 or b7)

- The notes C D E F G A B C naturally form a major scale. No #s or bs are needed.

- You can build a major scale on any note (e.g. G to G or D to D)

- All scales (other than C Major) require adjustment with sharps (or flats) to make them fit into the required pattern of tones and semitones. If a scale doesn't have a Tone, Tone, Semitone, Tone, Tone, Tone, Semitone pattern, it is *not* a major scale

- If you move in fifths (C – G – D – A – E etc.) building a major scale on each successive note requires you to add one new sharp

- The new sharp is always added on the 7th degree of each new major scale

We will look at the final three points from this list in much more detail in the next chapter, as they form the most important part of the Circle of Fifths.

Pop Quiz!

What is the pattern of tones and semitones in the major scale?

What is the master formula for the major scale?

Which major scale is built on the 5th note of C Major?

Which note do you sharpen when forming a new major scale on the 5th of the previous one?

How many sharps are there in the scale of G Major?

Chapter Three: Building the Circle of Fifths

As we saw in the previous chapter, the major scale always has the same set pattern of tones and semitones that must obeyed if the scale is to sound correct. This pattern is:

Tone, Tone, Semitone, Tone, Tone, Tone, Semitone.

We started with the scale of C Major because it has no sharps or flats.

C D E F G A B C

The next scale we built began on the 5th of the previous C Major scale = G.

G A B C D E F# G

We needed to raise the 7th note of the scale (to F#) to keep the required pattern of tones and semitones.

Let's continue this idea and build a scale on the 5th note of the G Major scale and see what happens.

(Remember to keep the F# we added in G Major)

The 5th of G is the note D. Building a scale from D to D, keeping the notes of the previous G Major scale gives us:

D E F# G A B C D.

Example 3a:

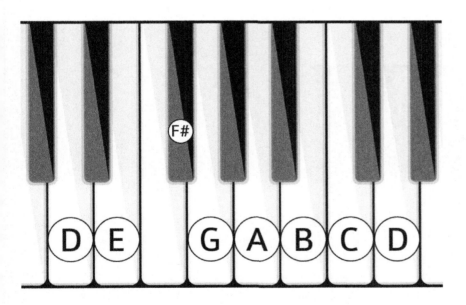

Ask yourself: is this a proper D Major scale?

The answer is no!

The distance between the 7th note (C) and the root (D) is a tone – just like it was in the previous chapter when we first formed a G scale by using the notes of C Major.

The step pattern of these notes is currently:

Tone, Tone, Semitone, Tone, Tone, **Semitone, Tone**.

What do we need to do to adjust this scale so it becomes a true major scale?

We need to raise the 7th to create the semitone distance between the 7th and the root.

We must raise the C to a C# to fix the pattern.

Example 3b:

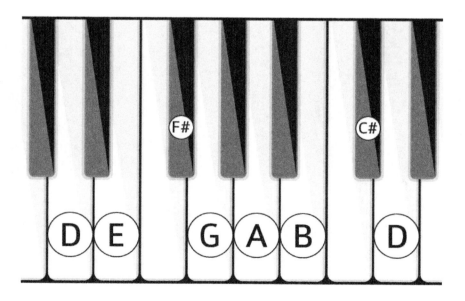

We have restored the Tone, Tone, Semitone, Tone, Tone, Tone, Semitone pattern and created a D Major scale.

This process is the essence of the Circle of Fifths.

We have learned that we can always build a new scale on the 5th of the previous one, and sharpen the 7th note in the new scale, to restore the correct distances between the notes to form a major scale.

Because of this process, the Circle of Fifths also tells us *how many sharps there are in any major scale*.

So, without further ado, let's start building the Circle of Fifths using what we know so far.

Starting with C at 12 o'clock, and moving clockwise, write out the sequence of fifths. If you're not sure of how to create this, refer back to chapter one.

The cycle of fifths is,

C G D A E B F# C#

Don't worry about the last two notes for now.

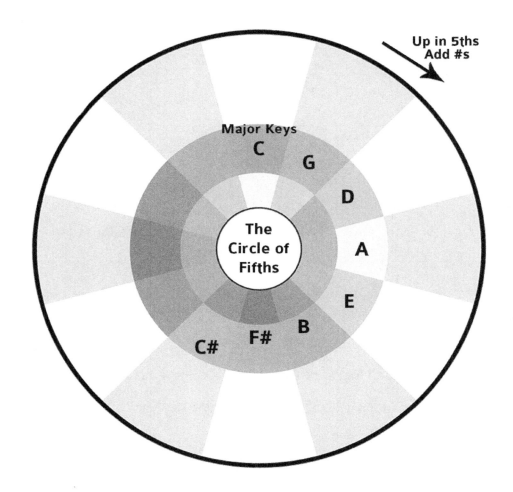

Next, in the outside segment, add in the number of #s used in each key:

Key	Scale	Number of #s
C Major	C D E F G A B C	0
G Major	G A B C D E F# G	1
D Major	D E F# G A B C# D	2
A Major	A B C# D E F# G# A	3
E Major	E F# G# A B C# D# E	4
B Major	B C# D# E F# G# A# B	5
F# Major	F# G# A# B C# D# E#	6
C# Major	C# D# E# F# G# A# B# C#	7

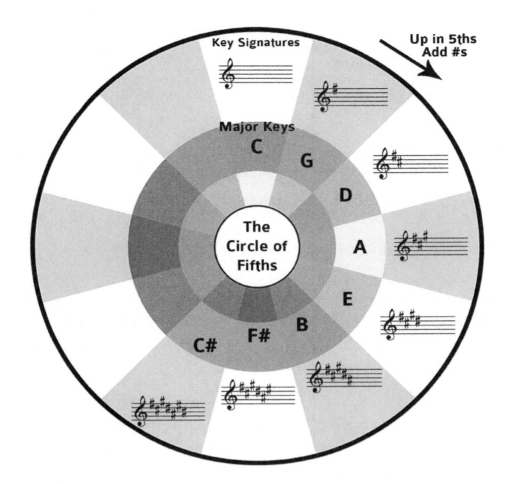

Notice that in the music notation the sharps are written on the stave in order of appearance.

The key signature for G Major shows one sharp, and it is written on the line F to show that the sharp added to the major scale is F#. This tells us that all the notes of G Major are the same as the notes in C Major, with the exception of the added F#.

The key signature of A Major shows three sharps in the order they are added. First we added F# to form G Major, then we added C# to form D Major, finally we added G# to form the A Major scale.

As you move clockwise around the diagram you can easily see how we add one sharp note each time to form a scale in a new key.

You can think of this trick as simply going up a semitone from the last sharp in the key signature to find the correct key.

For example:

The last sharp (on the right) in the above key signature is D#. Go up a semitone to find the key signature: E Major.

Check this on the Circle of Fifths diagram above and you will see that E Major has four sharps, and we were correct.

Top Tip! As the sharps are added *in the order they appear* to the key signature notation, the final sharp (on the right) is always a semitone below the key centre e.g. F# is a semitone below G.

Test yourself! What is the key shown by the following signatures? Look at the last sharp on the right and go up a semitone, then check your answer with the Circle of Fifths diagram above.

With practice, you will begin to remember how many sharps each key has. It can be useful to make some flash-cards to help you learn these more quickly.

The Order of Sharps

As we move clockwise through the Circle of Fifths, we always sharpen the seventh note of the new scale. This means that the order in which sharps appear as we move clockwise through key-centres is *always the same*.

One of the most useful things you can do is to memorise the following sequence of sharps:

F# - C# - G# - D# - A# - E# - B#

You could remember the sentence:

Funky **C**anadians **G**et **D**own **A**nd **E**at **B**ears!

Remember, the root/tonic of the scale is always a semitone above the last sharp, so if you see three sharps in a key signature like this:

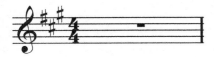

You will know that the sharps are F#, C# and G#, and the key is A Major because A is a semitone above G#.

Relative Minor Keys

Every major key has a closely related minor key/scale that contains all the same notes as the major scale, but starts in a different place in the scale. Finding the related minor scale is very similar to the way we found a new major key on the 5th of the previous one, but this time we do not alter any notes with sharps.

The *Relative Minor* is simply scale is built on the *sixth* note of any major scale.

Sometimes you will see it referred to as the Natural Minor scale, and you may even hear it called the Aeolian mode – but both are identical to the relative minor scale.

To form the relative/natural minor scale, simply go the sixth note of the major scale and begin a new scale from there.

For example, in C Major, the sixth note is an A:

1	2	3	4	5	6	7	1
C	D	E	F	G	A	B	C

To form the relative/natural minor scale, simply play the notes from A to A:

A Natural Minor:

1	2	3	4	5	6	7	1
A	B	C	D	E	F	G	A

No new sharps or flats are added. The A Natural Minor scale can be seen clearly in the following diagram:

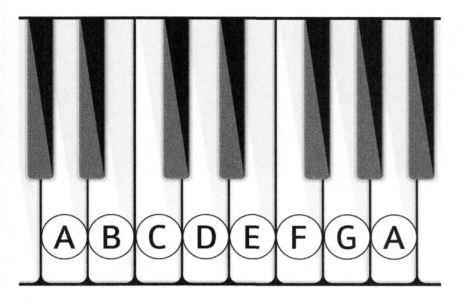

Without going off on a massive tangent on minor scale theory, it is important to understand the following points.

- Even though the natural minor scale contains the same notes as its relative major scale, it sounds completely different because it has a different pattern of tones and semitones

- The pattern of tones and semitones in the natural minor scale is Tone, Semitone, Tone, Tone, Semitone, Tone, Tone

- The first big difference between the major scale and the natural minor scale is that the distance between the *first* and *third* notes in the major scale is two tones, but only one-and-a-half tones in the natural minor scale. The distance of two tones is called a *major 3rd*. One-and-a-half tones is called a *minor 3rd*

- The second big difference is that in the major scale there is a semitone distance between the 7th note and the root. In the natural minor scale there is a distance of a tone between the 7th note and the root

See if you can see all these features of the natural minor scale in the diagram above.

Now, there are other types of minor scale – such as the melodic minor and harmonic minor scales – which are variations of the natural minor scale above. They are common in many types of music, but they are outside the scope of this book, so don't worry about them for now. It is enough to know that they exist.

Play through the A Natural Minor scale to understand its character. It may help to play an A Minor chord in your left hand to give the notes some musical context.

Example 3c:

While the major scale is bright and happy-sounding, the natural minor is quite sombre and dark. If you can't hear this right away, try playing the A Natural Minor scale over a sustained A Minor chord as in the audio example.

As natural minor scales contain exactly the same notes as their "parent" major scales, the two keys are very closely related, while sounding very different.

The keys of C Major and A Minor sound completely different, even though they contain the same notes. This is because the chords built on each scale have a kind of gravity that pulls back to the tonic chord (A or C).

Once again, we are moving into realms of theory that are outside the scope of this book. For now, you simply need to understand that we can use the relative minor key of any major key to create a closely related, albeit sad-sounding piece of music.

Bob Dylan's *All Along the Watchtower* was written using the natural minor scale, for instance.

As mentioned, you can find the relative minor key of any major key simply by counting up six notes of the scale.

For example, the relative minor of G Major is the key of E Minor:

1	2	3	4	5	6	7	1
G	A	B	C	D	E	F#	G

The relative minor of D Major is B Minor:

1	2	3	4	5	6	7	1
D	E	F#	G	A	B	C#	D

It's also really easy to move from a minor key to a relative major key. All you need to do is count *up* three scale notes.

What is the relative major key of A Minor?

1	2	3	4	5	6	7	1
A	B	**C**	D	E	F	G	A

The relative major of A Minor is C Major.

What is the relative major key of B Minor?

1	2	3	4	5	6	7	1
B	C#	**D**	E	F#	G#	A	B

The relative major of B Minor is D Major.

The relative major of a minor key is always four semitones above the root of the minor scale (include the starting note).

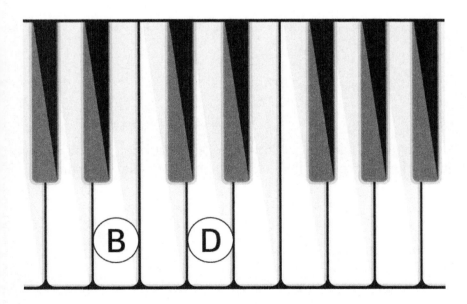

The absolutely essential point you need to know is this:

Major scales contain exactly the same notes as their relative natural minor scales. For this reason, *relative major and minor keys have exactly the same key signature.*

Because they contain the same notes:

The key of C Major has exactly the same key signature (0 sharps) as the key of A Minor

The key of G Major has exactly the same key signature (1 sharp) as the key of E Minor

The key of D Major has exactly the same key signature (2 sharps) as the key of B Minor

Often, the best way to tell whether a piece of music is written in the major or relative minor key is to look at the first chord.

If the key signature has one sharp and the first chord is a G Major, then the key is very likely to be G Major.

G Major

But if the key signature has one sharp and the first chord is E Minor, then the key is likely to be E Minor.

E Minor

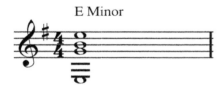

Now we understand how relative minor keys work, we can add them to the Circle of Fifths. relative minor keys sit next to their parent major keys on the inner circle. Note that relative majors and minors share the same key signature and number of sharps.

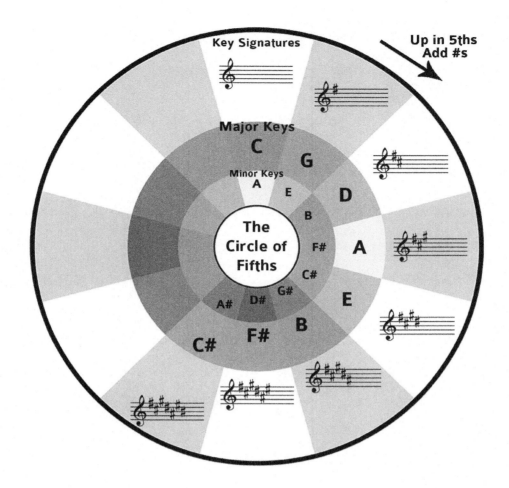

Once again, don't worry about the left hand side of this diagram, we will come to that soon.

Chapter Four: The Circle of Fourths

So far in this book, we have been forming new scales by moving *up* in 5ths, adding one sharp each time to create a new major scale.

There is another way to create the formula for a major scale without moving in 5ths and adding a sharp. We can also move in 4ths and add a flat.

In music, we can move between any two notes in different ways – by ascending *or* descending. For example, I can go from the note C to the note G by going *up* five notes (a 5th):

1	2	3	4	5
C	D	E	F	G

However, *ascending* a 5th, is actually the same as *descending* a 4th.

So I could move from C to G by going *down* four notes (a 4th).

1	2	3	4
C	B	A	G

Reversing the above idea tells us that:

Ascending a 4th takes us to the same note as *descending* a 5th.

For example, look at the Circle of Fifths diagram below. Start on the key of B Major and count the intervals between each key as you move counter-clockwise back towards C Major.

B Major to E Major:

B - C# - D# - E = a 4th.

42

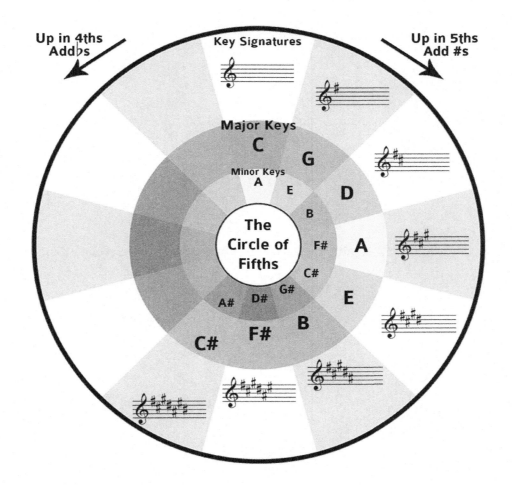

Keep following the circle counter-clockwise all the way to C.

E Major to A Major:

E - F# - G# - A = a 4th.

A Major to D Major:

A - B – C# - D = a 4th.

This pattern continues all the way back to C Major. But what happens if we keep going?

The note a 4th above (5th below) C is F.

1	2	3	4
C	D	E	F

What happens if we build a scale on F using the notes of the C Major scale?

We get the notes:

1	2	3	4	5	6	7	1
F	G	A	B	C	D	E	F

Let's look at the pattern of tones and semitones formed by these notes to see if they make a true major scale.

F to G = Tone

G to A = Tone

A to B = Tone

B to C = Semitone

C to D = Tone

D to E = Tone

E to F = Semitone

On the piano, this pattern of notes looks and sounds like this:

Example 4a:

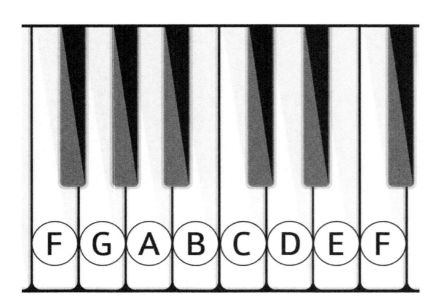

The pattern of these notes is

Tone, Tone, **Tone**, **Semitone**, Tone, Tone, Semitone

This does *not* currently form a major scale. There is a problem between the third and fourth notes.

Remember, the pattern of the major scale is,

Tone, Tone, **Semitone**, **Tone**, Tone, Tone, Semitone.

Can you see where we could change just one note to turn this F-to-F pattern into a true major scale?

If we flatten the fourth note (B) of this "F" scale so that it becomes Bb, we correct the pattern of tones and semitones so it becomes a true major scale. The notes are now:

1	2	3	4	5	6	7
F	G	A	Bb	C	D	E

And the pattern of tones and Semitones is now Tone, Tone, Semitone, Tone, Tone, Tone, Semitone.

Example 4b:

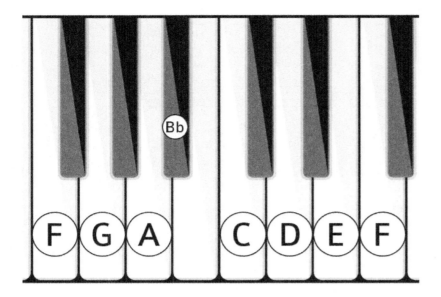

We have created a major scale by ascending a 4th from the previous scale (C Major) and flattening the fourth note of the scale. This movement is the essence of the Circle of Fourths and is how we move between keys when going *counter-clockwise* around the Circle of Fifths diagram. Our diagram now looks like this:

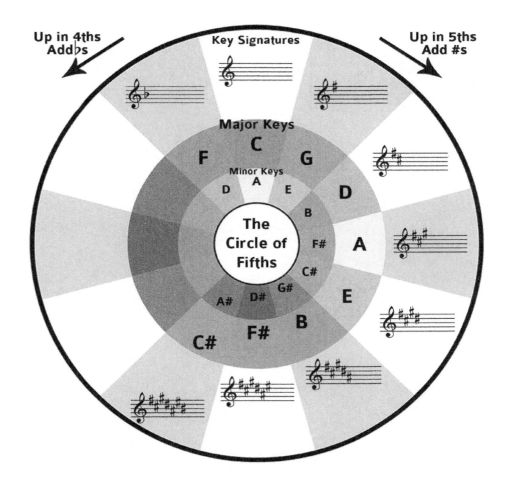

The relative minor of F Major (the scale built on the sixth note) is D Minor, so I have added this into the diagram too.

I have also added the key signature for F Major/D Minor to the diagram. The scale of F Major/D Minor contains one flat (the note Bb) and the key signature looks like this when notated:

Let's repeat the process and find the key and scale created when we move counter-clockwise round the Circle of Fifths from F Major.

A 4th above (or a 5th below) F is the note Bb. (Remember, the Bb was added in the previous example).

1	2	3	4
F	G	A	Bb

First, we build a new scale on the note Bb:

1	2	3	4	5	6	7
Bb	C	D	E	F	G	A

Check to see that the pattern of tones and semitones does *not* form a major scale. The pattern above is

Tone, Tone, Tone, Semitone, Tone, Tone, Semitone.

To correct the pattern, we once again need to flatten the fourth note of the scale. In this case, that note is Eb:

1	2	3	4	5	6	7
Bb	C	D	Eb	F	G	A

The patterns of tones and semitones is now correct and forms a true Major scale:

Bb to C = Tone

C to D = Tone

D to Eb = Semitone

Eb to F = Tone

F to G = Tone

G to A = Tone

A to Bb = Semitone

Again, we can add this scale of Bb Major and its relative minor (G Minor) to our diagram.

As you can see in the above table, the key signature of Bb Major/G Minor contains two flats, and these are the notes Bb and Eb. They are placed on the stave in the order they appeared in the cycle of fourths.

48

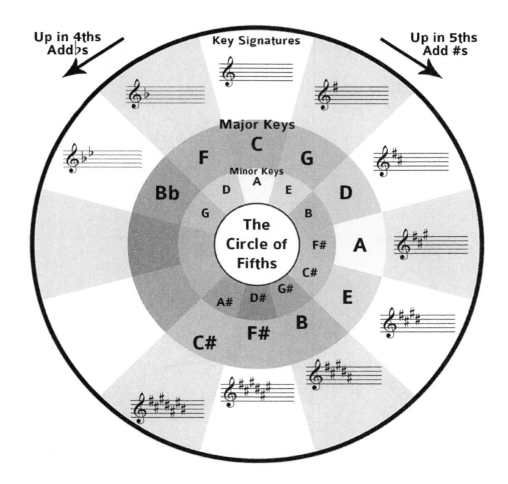

Major Keys
C
F   G
Minor Keys
A
D   E
Bb
G   B
The
Circle of   F#
Fifths
C#
G#
A#   D#
E
C#   F#   B

Let's quickly recap the rule of the Cycle of Fourths.

You can create a new major scale by building a new scale on the fourth note of the previous scale, then flattening the fourth note of the new scale.

Use this rule to easily complete the rest of the Circle of Fifths.

The last scale we built was Bb Major.

The fourth note of Bb Major is Eb.

Build a new scale from Eb and flatten the fourth note:

1	2	3	4	5	6	7
Eb	F	G	Ab	Bb	C	D

The relative minor (built on the sixth note) is C Minor.

The key signature contains three flats and, once again, they are placed on the stave in the order they appeared in the cycle.

49

The next major scale/key built on the fourth of Eb is Ab Major. Build the scale and flatten the fourth:

1	2	3	4	5	6	7
Ab	Bb	C	Db	Eb	F	G

The relative minor is F Minor.

Continue this sequence and add all these keys to complete the diagram.

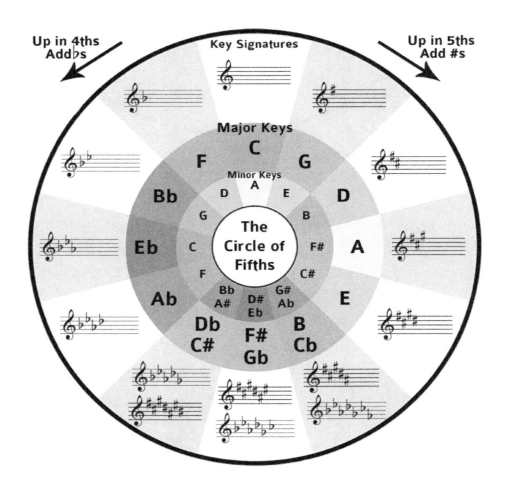

Notice that when moving in 4ths, the next scale is always built on the note that was flattened in the previous key. For example, the note that was flattened in the key of F was Bb. The next scale in the cycle of 4ths is Bb Major. Don't worry about there being two keys in the bottom three segments. This will be explained soon.

The Order of Flats

Just as with sharps, flats are always added in a particular pattern.

As we move counter-clockwise round the circle from C, we always flatten the fourth note of the new scale. This means that the order in which flats appear as we move counter-clockwise through key-centres is *always the same*.

Again, one of the most useful things you can do is to memorise the following sequence of flats:

Bb, Eb, Ab, Db, Gb, Cb, Fb

You could remember the sentence:

Beans **E**aten **A**t **D**inner **G**et **C**harlie **F**arty

Notice that the order of flats B E A D G C F is the opposite to the order of sharps F C G D A E B, which makes sense as you will learn in the "Moving Around the Circle" section below.

Enharmonic Keys

You will notice that the three key signatures at the bottom of the Circle of Fifths have two names and two key signatures. Don't panic! This is easy to explain once you understand how *enharmonic* notes work.

Enharmonic is just a fancy way to say "two names".

You may already know some enharmonic note names. For example, the note C# is identical to the note Db.

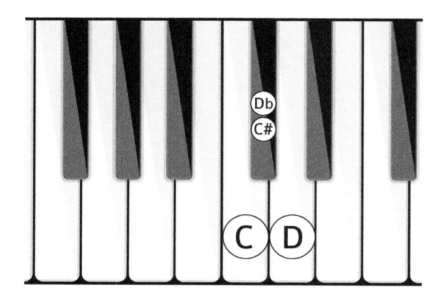

Going *up* a semitone from C is the same as going *down* a semitone from D.

In other words, if we sharpen the note C we get the note C#, and if we flatten the note D, we get Db.

C# and Db are the same note.

Other enharmonic notes pairs are:

D# and Eb

F# and Gb

G# and Ab

A# and Bb

The distance between the notes E and F is only a semitone, so it is very rare to see the notes E# or Fb.

The distance between the notes B and C is only a semitone, so it is very rare to see the notes B# or Cb.

However, these notes do theoretically occur, and you will understand why when you consider how we formed the Circle of Fifths. If we move far enough in any direction, eventually *all* the notes of the scale can be come sharpened or flattened.

In fact, you will see that F# Major contains the note E# because E it is the seventh note of the scale and it always needs to be sharpened to form a semitone between the 7th note of the scale and the root (as you saw in the Circle of Fifths clockwise section).

The scale of C# Major contains the notes of both E# and B# for the same reason.

But also… think about it!… The key of C Major contains no sharps, so to form the major scale formula from the note C# we must need to sharpen *every* note in the scale!

However, to see keys that contain this terrifying number of sharps and flats is rare for a number of reasons.

Firstly, why would you write a piece of music in the key of C# Major when you could simply write it in a more common key such as C Major or D Major, which would be much easier to read? The idea of music notation is to convey musical ideas as quickly and as cleanly as possible. If someone hands you a piece of music to read in F# Major or C# Major, you may want to have a quiet word with them!

Secondly, it is possible to use enharmonics to write a complex key signature much more simply.

We know that the note C# is identical to the note Db, so if you do find yourself having to write in C# Major, why not write in Db Major instead? I know I'd much prefer to see five flats than seven sharps.

The three keys at the bottom of the Circle of Fifths show two ways of writing exactly the same thing. For example, the notes in C# Major are identical to the notes in Db Major.

Look for enharmonic spellings in the table below to illustrate this important point:

Scale	1	2	3	4	5	6	7
C# Major	C#	D#	E#	F#	G#	A#	B#
Db Major	Db	Eb	F	Gb	Ab	Bb	C

In theory you can use the concept of enharmonic notes to move indefinitely around the circle in either direction, but in practice this becomes very complex after the keys of F# and Gb.

Generally, the left-hand side of the diagram is used to reference "flat" keys and the right hand side of the table is used to reference "sharp" keys.

Moving around the Circle in Both Directions

One final, important thing to note is that if you are on the "sharp" (right-hand) side of the circle and you want to move counter-clockwise (for example from A Major to D Major) you simply reverse the process used when you built the scale of D Major on the 5th of A Major.

To move from A Major to D Major, go *down* a 5th (up a 4th) and remove (flatten) the sharp you previously added (G#).

To move from G Major to C Major, go *down* a 5th (up a 4th) and remove (flatten) the sharp you previously added (F#).

Each time you move counter-clockwise round the Circle of Fifths, you ascend a 4th and flatten the 7th note of the scale you start on (the 7th of G is F#).

This process continues to work as you move past C Major.

Move to the 4th of C Major (F) and flatten the 7th of the starting scale (the 7th of C Major is Bb).

Check that the key of F Major has the notes of C Major except for a Bb.

Moving counter-clockwise from F Major to Bb Major uses the same process.

The fourth of Bb Major is Eb.

The scale of Bb Major contains the notes of Eb Major, except for the Eb. (The 7th note of the starting F Major scale was E).

The rule is:

To move counter-clockwise from *anywhere* on the Circle of Fifths, go up a 4th and flatten the final note.

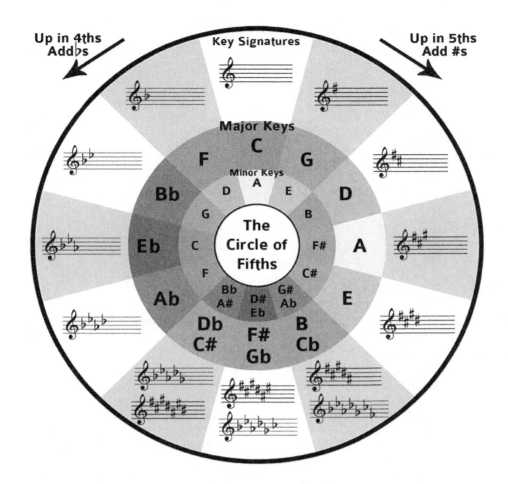

Don't forget that when you flatten any # note (for example G#) it becomes a *natural* note. i.e. G# becomes a G when you flatten it.

The procedure works when we wish to move *clockwise* from the *flat* (left-hand) side of the circle. For example, moving from Ab Major to Eb Major.

When we move clockwise from the "flat" side of the circle, we always ascend a 5th and sharpen the last flat that was added.

For example, moving from Ab Major to Eb Major:

The fifth of Ab Major is Eb Major.

Sharpen the final flat that was added to the key signature of Ab Major (Db).

Now you have the scale/key of Eb Major.

Remember from earlier that the flat added as you move counter-clockwise from C Major was always the 4th note of the scale, so this is the note we are sharpening now as we move clockwise.

Using this idea, we can continue clockwise past C Major and form G Major.

The 5th of C Major is G.

Sharpen the 4th of C Major (F) to create the F# needed for the scale of G Major.

The two methods written above are just a couple of different ways you can think about moving between keys. They help sometimes, but might be a little confusing at first. As you become more familiar with the circle, you will find that you naturally start to figure these little tricks out for yourself.

Generally, remember the following rules:

- To move clockwise: go up a 5th and add a sharp

- To move counter-clockwise: go up a 4th and remove a sharp

How to Use the Circle of Fifths

At this point you should have a good understanding of the following ideas.

- The Circle of Fifths tells us the notes in any major or minor key

- The Circle of Fifths moves both clockwise or counter-clockwise (circle of fourths)

- Moving clockwise from C gives us the "sharp" keys

- To move clockwise, build a scale on the fifth of the previous one and sharpen the 7th

- Moving counter-clockwise from C gives us the "flat" keys

- To move counter-clockwise, build a scale on the fourth of the previous one and flatten the 4th

You may well be asking yourself, "What's the point of knowing all this?!"

It's a good question, because really the Circle of Fifths is a completely theoretical tool. It simply tells us which notes are in any given key.

But, if you were writing a song, and the singer was restricted to a particular vocal range, the circle may come in quite handy then.

If the singer says, "I can only sing in the key of E Major", all you need to do is look at the circle to see which notes are in that key.

The key of E Major has four sharps: F#, C#, G# and D#, so the notes in that key are:

E F# G# A B C# and D#

Remember that the final sharp in the sequence (D#) is always a semitone below the key centre (in this case E Major).

So, other than quickly telling us the key signature and notes of any major or minor scale or key, what has the Circle of Fifths ever done for us?

Well, actually, the Circle of Fifths is a really important reference tool when *writing* music.

As you probably know, music often changes key or *modulates*. The thing is, if the music jumps to a key that isn't closely related, the key change can sound obvious or even a little awkward.

Sometimes a very obvious key change is exactly what you want, and sudden key changes do often happen as a great effect in music.

Check out Earth Wind and Fire's *After the Love Has Gone*, The Who's *My Generation*, R.E.M.'s *Stand*, or Whitney Houston's *I Will Always Love You* for some seriously powerful key changes.

The best rock key change in music is clearly Bon Jovi's *Livin' on a Prayer* where the key changes up a minor 3rd! Check it out near the end of the song.

However, we don't always want the modulation to be so obvious and many writers (especially early classical/baroque composers like Bach, Handel and Mozart) want to make their key changes so subtle they are barely noticeable to the listener. They want to take the audience on a subtle musical journey that they *feel* rather than become consciously aware of. To do this, composers regularly make small modulations by adjusting just one or two notes in the scales or harmony they are using to create the music.

As we know, moving around the Circle of Fifths in either direction shows us how we can adjust just one note in order to change to a very closely related key.

Look at the Circle of Fifths now and focus on the key of A Major (which has three sharps).

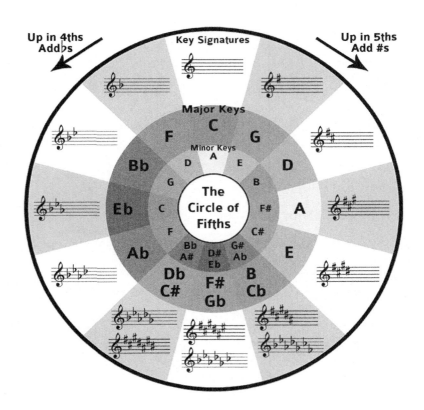

Which keys can we move to, by changing just one note?

If you answered "two", you're nearly correct. We can add or remove a sharp to move to the closely related keys of D Major and E Major, but don't forget the relative minors!

In fact, there are always *five* closely related keys that can be reached from any key centre, just by moving clockwise or counter-clockwise through the Circle of Fifths.

We can use:

- The relative minor of the current key

- The clockwise key and its relative minor

- The counter-clockwise key and its relative minor

So from the key of A Major, we can move smoothly to the five keys of:

- F# Minor

- E Major

- C# Minor

- D Major

- B Minor

Four of these keys are just a note change away from the original key of A Major, and we don't actually have to change *any* notes to move to the key of F# Minor.[1]

A couple of important words to describe key changes

In music you will often hear the terms *Dominant* and *Subdominant*.

- Dominant chords (or keys) are built on the 5th note of a scale

- Subdominant chords (or keys) are built on the 4th note of the scale

So…

The dominant chord (or key) of A Major is E Major.

The subdominant chord (or key) of A Major is D Major.

When we move clockwise around the Circle of Fifths, we build a new scale on the dominant (5th) note of the current scale.

When we move counter-clockwise around the Circle of Fifths we build a new scale on the subdominant (4th) note of the current scale.

Sometimes you will hear musicians saying things that seem complex like, "modulate to the subdominant…"

All that really means is that we are changing key to the scale built on the 4th note of the key – or simply moving counter-clockwise one step. For example, changing from the key of A Major to the key of D Major.

You may hear a statement like, "The composer modulated to the dominant's relative minor…"

This simply means that the composer changed key to the relative minor of the key built on the 5th step of the scale. Or, simply that they moved one clockwise step round the circle and used the relative minor scale instead of the major scale.

---

1. In practice, the natural minor form of the relative minor scale is rarely used, and instead it is more common to use the melodic and harmonic minor scales to form melody and harmony. These two scales do add extra sharps and flats, but the study of this kind of music theory is well outside the scope of this book.

For example, if we were in the key of A Major, the dominant key is E Major (the 5th). The relative minor of E Major is C# Minor. The composer changed key from A Major to C# Minor.

Follow the above ideas through on the Circle of Fifths diagram to make sure you understand this kind of terminology.

Some musicians have a habit of trying to sound smart to confuse mere mortal non-musicians! Once you understand a few pieces of important terminology, you'll find that it really isn't that hard to communicate musically.

A detailed exploration of the actual process of changing keys would demand a (long) book to itself, and unfortunately it's outside the scope of this book that focuses on the Circle of Fifths. However, as a quick overview, and hopefully to get you being creative, here is a very quick, broad overview of how it all works.

To make chords from scales we simply stack three or more notes on each scale tone. Normally these notes are a 3rd and a 5th above the scale tone.

For example, using the scale of A Major:

1	2	3	4	5	6	7
A	B	C#	D	E	F#	G#

Example 4c:

Don't forget, the sharps are written in the key signature!

To harmonise the first note (A), I would use the notes a 3rd and a 5th above (C# and E).

The first chord in the key of A Major therefore contains the notes A, C# and E. These notes form an A Major chord.

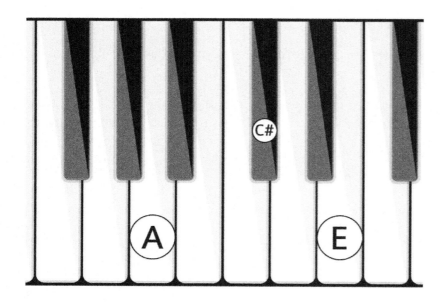

To harmonise the second note (B) I would once again use the notes a 3rd and a 5th above the root, so the second chord in A Major contains the notes B, D and F#. This is a B Minor chord.

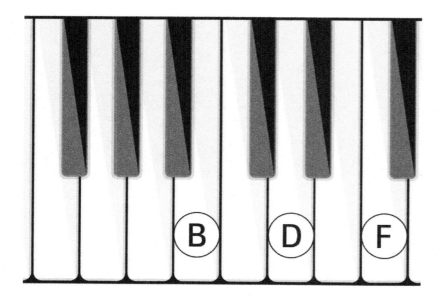

(Major chords have two tones between the root and 3rd. Minor chords have a tone-and-a-half between the root and the 3rd).

Continuing this process, we get the following chords in the key of A Major:

A Major:

Chord Number	Chord	Spelling
1	A Major	A C# E
2	B Minor	B D F#
3	C# Minor	C# E G#
4	D Major	D F# A
5	E Major	E G# B
6	F# Minor	F# A C#
7	G# Diminished[2]	G# B D

We can play these chords on the piano in the following way:

Example 4d:

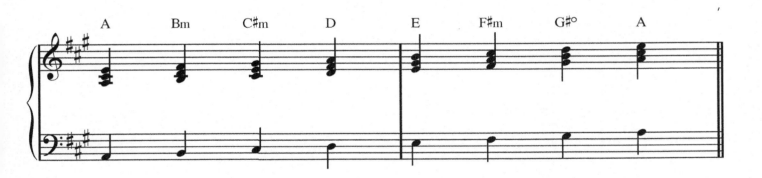

The important thing to understand when changing key is that each of the five closely-related keys we mentioned earlier contain some chords that are the same as in A Major, and some chords that are different.

This shouldn't be a surprise, because we already know that there is only one note (D#) different between the two keys.

For example, here are the chords that are in the key of E Major (the dominant key of A Major).

E Major:

Chord Number	Chord	Spelling
1	E Major	E G# B
2	F# Minor	F# A C#
3	G# Minor	G# B D#
4	A Major	A C# E
5	B Major	B D# F#
6	C# Minor	C# E G#
7	D# Diminished	D# F# A

Example 4e:

The keys of A Major and E Major actually have four chords in common and only three chords that are different.

Chord number 1 of A Major is the same as chord number 4 of E Major.

Look to see which chords the two keys have in common, and which are different.

In fact, as we have only changed one note (D to D#) between these two keys, it should make sense that only the chords that contain a D in the key of A Major will change when we move to E Major.

Here is a simple musical example that uses the Circle of Fifths to modulate *twice* from A Major. I use different inversions to create smooth movements between the chords, but none of the notes have been changed from the simple triad.

Example 4f:

The example begins in A Major and stays there for the first seven bars. The chord B Major is used to mark a very clear movement into E Major in bar eight (B Major is chord 5 in the key of E Major, and is the first chord played that doesn't exist in the key of A Major).

Is the F# Minor chord 2 in E Major, or is it chord 6 in A Major?! Well, it's both! In this example the F# Minor is used to pivot between the two keys.

The second eight bars repeat exactly the same chord progression, but this time in the key of E Major. In bar sixteen, the F# Major chord functions in the same way as the B Major chord did in bar eight. The F# Major chord does *not* exist in the previous key of E Major, and is instead chord 5 of a new key: B Major. (Add a B Major chord to the end of the above sequence to hear the modulation "resolve" into the new key.

As with the F# Minor chord in bar seven, the C# Minor chord in bar fifteen is the pivot chord. It exists in both the keys E Major (chord 6) and B Major (chord 2). It is played before the B Major in bar sixteen to "smooth the way" into the modulation to the dominant.

Once again, the chord progression modulated one key *clockwise* around the Circle of Fifths.

The movement of keys went:

A – E – B. Make sure you can follow this idea round on the Circle of Fifths.

This idea of "pivot chords" works in the same way when modulating to any of the five closely-related keys.

For example, moving counter-clockwise around the circle from A Major, and modulating to the subdominant key of D Major, the same thing occurs.

Refer back to the Circle of Fifths and you will see that only note changes between A Major and D Major. The G# of A Major becomes a G natural in D Major. (Remember, when we move anti-clockwise round the Circle of Fifths, we remove one sharp)

A Major:

1	2	3	4	5	6	7
A	B	C#	D	E	F#	G#

D Major:

1	2	3	4	5	6	7
D	E	F#	G	A	B	C#

When changing from A Major to D Major, only the chords that contained a G# in A Major will change in D Major. Once again, there are four identical chords and three new chords.

D Major:

Chord Number	Chord	Spelling
1	D Major	D F# A
2	E Minor	E G B
3	F# Minor	F# A C#
4	G Major	G B D
5	A Major	A C# E
6	B Minor	B D F#
7	C# Diminished	C# E G

Here are the harmonised chords in D Major.

Example 4g:

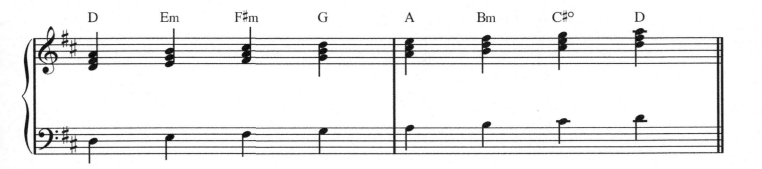

Once again, compare the above table to the table of chords in A Major and look to see which chords change and which stay the same.

For example, chord 6 in D Major is the same as chord 2 in A Major.

Here's a simple example that shows a modulation from A Major to D Major. See if you can spot the first chord that exists in D Major but not in A Major, and notice the pivot chord that precedes the key change.

Example 4h:

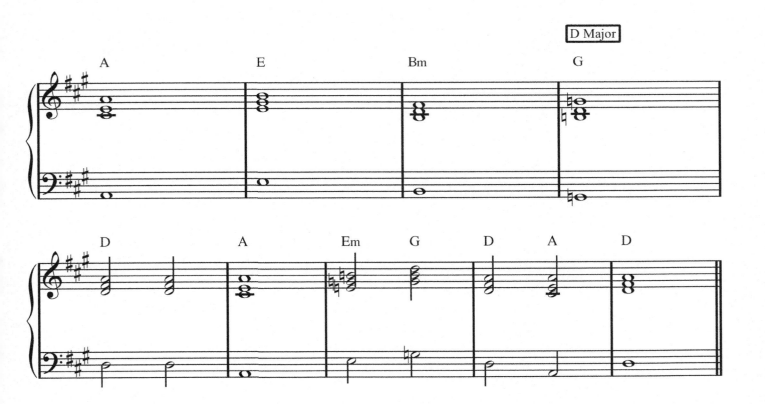

In the above example, the key change to D Major in announced in bar seven by the use of the G Major chord. G Major is chord 4 in the key of D Major, but doesn't exist in the starting key of A Major. The chord of B Minor is the pivot that is contained in both keys. B Minor is chord 2 in A Major and chord 6 in D Major.

To summarise the whole complex subject of modulation in a few paragraphs:

When changing key, composers use the Circle of Fifths to find all the chords that are identical and different between two keys. The identical chords are called *pivots* because they are used to "pivot" between the two keys when modulating. For example, I could use chord 6 of D Major (B Minor) to pivot or "bridge" between the keys of D Major and A Major, because B Minor is *also* chord 2 in A Major.

The listener doesn't even know that the key change has happened *until* I write a chord (or melody note) from A Major that is different from any of the chords (or notes) in D Major.

For example, the chord E Major is a very important chord in the key of A Major, but it doesn't exist in the key of D Major. When the listener hears the chord of E Major, they hear the new note (G#) and realise that something has changed and that the music has modulated away from the original key of D Major.

Modulation is a huge, complex subject that is barely covered by most university degrees in music, so don't worry if you have a few questions after that mini explanation! The idea was just to show you that the Circle of Fifths is an important reference to tell us not only how each scale and key is created, but also to tell us how closely each key is *related*.

The key to a successful understanding of the Circle of Fifths is to practice building it yourself from the beginning. Along with the audio downloads, I have included an empty Circle of Fifths diagram for you to print out and use to help you practise this important concept in music.

You can download it from:

www.fundamental-changes.com and it is included in the audio download file for this book.

The only way to learn and truly understand music is to get your hands dirty and dive right in. Grab a pencil and keep building the circle until you can't get it wrong.

Have fun!

Joseph

First Steps in Classical Piano

Take Your First Steps in Classical Piano Playing

First Steps in Classical Piano is the beginning of your journey to playing beautiful classical piano pieces.

Either as a stand-alone guide, or as a resource to support lessons with your piano teacher, this book will dramatically speed up how you learn to play piano.

You will quickly master excerpts from iconic classical piano pieces, while learning to read music, play scales and develop piano technique.

If you love the sound of classical piano, but thought it would be too hard to learn, think again.

This book explains in simple language the fundamentals you need to know to play beautiful piano pieces and includes lessons on how to develop correct technique, navigate the keyboard and read music notation.

You will master three simple scale patterns that unlock the melodies of famous classical piano pieces and work towards playing longer pieces by the end of the book.

What you'll learn:

• How to navigate the piano keyboard

• How to read music notation

• The three major scale patterns that unlock famous pieces by Strauss, Mozart, Brahms, Haydn and Beethoven

• Perfect piano technique from the ground up

• How to recognise keys and play in different time signatures

• How chords are formed and used in classical piano

Other Books from Fundamental Changes

Printed in Great Britain
by Amazon